THE IMPACTS OF COVID-19 PANDEMIC ON INTERNATIONAL TRADE, ECONOMY, TOURISM, PEACE AND SECURITY WITH A SPECIAL REFERENCE TO INDIA

RITURAJ BASUMATARY | SWMAOSHAR BRAHMA

Contents

Preface

This book deals with the impacts of COVID-19 pandemic on International Trade, Economy, Tourism, Peace & Security with a special reference to India. Hope that the publication of this book will be useful. This book may not be free from errors and constructive criticisms are welcomed for the improvement of this book.

The impacts of COVID-19 pandemic on International Trade, Economy, Tourism, Peace & Security with a special reference to India
Rituraj Basumatary
Swmaoshar Brahma

Abstract

At the height of the COVID-19 pandemic's first wave in the mid-2020, we were living the first phase of the COVID-19 virus. It was a relatively new virus and a public health crisis which left governments scrambling to lockdown and the public sector in different countries of the world largely failed. At present, the vaccines for the COVID-19 are out and we are in the second phase of the pandemic. Vaccines for the coronavirus, some using innovative mRNA techniques and developed by international teams have begun rolling out which we had never seen before. The death rates has decreased to a certain extent and new and cheaper tests are being developed each month. As we have entered the second phase of the crisis, which will be led by the dynamism, innovation and competence of the private sector. There are still challenges of distribution of the vaccine due to the huge overcrowded population in our country. But on the horizon, a true post-pandemic world is now in sight.

The private sector has delivered the vaccines, but we should not forget the indispensable role that the state played in funding vaccine research and development at a fast speed. Only in East Asia and a few other countries of the world, we have seen an effective public and private sector response.

With the exception of a stressed financial sector, India went into the coronavirus crisis with sound economic fundamentals. The lockdown in response to the threat of the virus created unprecedented friction in transactions between buyers and sellers of goods and services as well as of inputs. The lockdown has created a lot of difficulties specially for the backward classes people.

Keywords:- Micro-economic, Impacts, COVID-19, Pandemic, Coronavirus.

CHAPTER I

Introduction

Coronavirus disease 2019(COVID-19) is an infectious disease caused by severe acute respiratory syndrome coronavirus 2(SARS-COV-2). The disease was first identified in 2019 in Wuhan, the capital of China's Hubei province, and has since spread globally, resulting in the 2019-2020 coronavirus pandemic. Common symptoms include fever, cough, and shortness of breath. Other symptoms may include muscle pain, sputum production, diarrhoea, sore throat, abdominal pain, and loss of smell or taste. While the majority of cases result in mild symptoms, some progress to pneumonia and multi-organ failure. As of March 25, 2020, the overall rate of deaths per number of diagnosed cases is 4.5 percent; ranging from 0.2 percent to 15 percent according to age group and other health problems. The virus is mainly spread during close contact and via respiratory droplets produced when people cough or sneeze. Respiratory droplets may be produced during breathing but the virus is not considered airborne. People may also catch COVID-19 by touching a contaminated surface and then their face. It is more contagious when people are symptomatic, although spread may be possible before symptoms appear. The virus can live on surfaces up to 72 hours. Time from exposure to onset of symptoms is generally between two and fourteen days, with an average of five days. The standard method of diagnosis is by five days. The standard method of diagnosis is by reverse transcription polymerase chain reaction (rRTPCR) from a nasopharyngeal swab. The infection can also be diagnosed from a combination of symptoms, risk factors and a chest CT scan showing features of pneumonia.

Recommended measures to prevent infection include frequent hand washing, social distancing (maintaining physical distance from others, especially from those with symptoms), covering coughs and sneezes with a tissue or inner elbow, and keeping unwashed hands away from the face. The use of masks is recommended by some national health authorities for those who suspect they have the virus and their caregivers, but not for the general public, although simple cloth masks may be use by those who desire them. There is no vaccine or specific antiviral treatment for COVID-19. Management involves treatment of symptoms, supportive care, isolation and experimental measures.

The World Health Organisation (WHO) declared the 2019-2020 coronavirus outbreak a Public Health Emergency of International Concern (PHEIC) on 30 January 2020 and a pandemic on 11 March 2020. Local transmission of the disease has been recorded in many countries across all six WHO regions.

Most people infected with the COVID-19 virus will experience mild to moderate respiratory illness and recover without requiring special treatment. Older people, and those with underlying medical problems like cardiovascular disease, diabetes, chronic respiratory disease and cancer are more likely to develop serious illness.

The best way to prevent and slow down transmission is be well informed about the COVID-19 virus, the disease it causes and how it spreads. Protect yourself and others from infection by washing your hands or using an alcohol based rub frequently and not touching your face.

The COVID-19 virus spreads primarily through droplets of saliva or discharge from the nose when an infected person coughs or sneezes, so it's important that you also practice respiratory etiquette (for example, by coughing into a flexed elbow).

At this time, there are no specific vaccines or treatments for COVID-19. However, there are many ongoing clinical trials evaluating potential treatments. WHO will continue to provide updated information as soon as clinical findings become available.

COVID-19 is thought to have originated in a seafood market where wildlife was sold illegally. On February 7, 2020, Chinese researchers said the virus could have spread from an infected animal to humans through illegally trafficked pangolins, prized in Asia for food and medicine. Scientists have pointed to either bats or snakes as possible sources.

CHAPTER II

Impacts of COVID-19 on Global Trade

Besides its worrying effects on human life, the novel strain of coronavirus has the potential to significantly slow down the global economy. Several industries have been adversely impacted due to the spread of COVID-19 globally. It is evident that the global economy is grinding to a halt. As business close to help prevent transmission of COVID-19, financial concerns and job losses are one of the first human impacts of the virus.

We have seen the significant economic impact of the coronavirus on financial markets and vulnerable industries such as manufacturing, tourism, hospitality and travel. Travel and tourism account for 10 % of the global GDP and 50 million jobs are at risk worldwide. Global tourism, travel and hospitality companies closing down affects SMEs globally.

Responding to the crisis requires global cooperation among governments, international organisations and the business community, which is at the centre of the World Economic Forum's mission as the International Organization for Public-Private Cooperation.

The Forum has created the COVID Action Platform, a global platform to convene the business community for collective action, protect people's livelihoods and facilitate business continuity, and mobilize support for the COVID-19 response. The platform is created with the support of the World Health Organisation and is open to all businesses and industry groups, as well as other stakeholders, aiming to integrate and inform joint action.

As an organisation, the Forum has a track record of supporting efforts to contain epidemics.

CHAPTER III

Impacts of COVID-19 on Global Education

Over a billion students worldwide are unable to go to school or university, due to measures to stop the spread of COVID-19. The pandemic is expected to have a huge impact on global education.

According to UNESCO monitoring, over 100 countries have implemented nationwide closures, impacting nearly 90 % of the world's student population. School closures impact not only students, teachers and families, but have farreaching economic and societal consequences. School closures in response to COVID-19 have shed light on various social and economic issues, including student debt, digital learning, food insecurity, and homelessness, as well as access to child care, health care, housing, internet and disability services.

Efforts to stem the spread of COVID-19 through non-pharmaceutical interventions and preventive measures such as social-distancing and self-isolation have prompted the widespread closure of primary, secondary, and tertiary schooling in over 100 countries.

CHAPTER IV

Impacts of COVID-19 on World Tourism

The World Travel and Tourism Council has warned the COVID-19 pandemic could cut 50 million jobs worldwide in the travel and tourism industry. Asia is expected to be the worst affected continent and once the outbreak is over, it could take up to 10 months for the industry to recover. The tourism industry currently accounts for about 10 % of global GDP. The coronavirus epidemic is putting up to 50 million jobs in the global travel and tourism sector at risk, with travel likely to slump by a quarter this year. This impact would depend on how long the epidemic lasts and could still be exacerbated by recent restrictive measures; such as those taken by the U.S. administration on travel to Europe.

Around 850,000 people travel each month from Europe to the United States, equivalent to a $ 3.4 billion monthly contribution to the U.S. economy. Of the 50 million jobs that could be lost, it is expected that around 30 million would be in Asia, seven million in Europe, five million in the Americas and the rest in other continents.

CHAPTER V

COVID-19 as a threat to International Peace and Security

Security generally means freedom from threats. There are two notions of Security:- (I) Traditional and (II) non-Traditional notions of Security.

Traditional conceptions of security are generally concerned with the use, threat of use, or of military force. In the traditional conception of security, the greatest danger to a country is from military threats.

Non-Traditional notions of security go beyond military threat to cover a big range of threats endanger affected the conditions of human existence. Non-Traditional views of security have been termed 'human-security' or 'global-security'.

In the broad concept of human security, the threat agenda should cover hunger, poverty, natural disasters, hence, these kill for more people than war. In its broadest formulation, the very human activity index accompanied human securities and threats of human dignity.

The very idea of Global Security emerged in the 1990's in response to the global nature of threats i.e. global warming, health epidemic etc. Since the very problems are global in nature, hence, international co-operation is necessary.

The rapid spread of COVID-19 and actions to contain the virus have understandably drawn parallels with previous outbreaks, in particular that of Ebola in 2014 and of the outbreak of Severe Acute Respiratory Syndrome

(SARS) in 2003 which also arose in China but affected Hong Kong more severely. While the SARS outbreak went largely unnoticed (at least not formally) by the Security Council, in 2014, it designated the Ebola outbreak in West Africa as a threat to international peace and security. Resolution 2177(2014) was the first time the Security Council had considered and subsequently determined a public health issue a threat to international peace and security in line with Article 39 of the UN Charter. This post examines briefly the Security Council's response to the Ebola outbreak and considers whether a comparable response may result towards the currently COVID-19 outbreak. First, it assesses factors for the Security Council's designation of the Ebola outbreak as a threat to peace and security are comparable to the current coronavirus outbreak. And third, it highlights some legal aspects pertaining to such a designation, including potential effects of that designation.

The COVID-19 has affected more than 200 countries and territories around the world and 2 international conveyances: the Diamond Princess Cruise Ship harboured in Yokohama, Japan, and the Holland America's Cruise Ship.

CHAPTER VI

COVID-19 and India

Though India has done well in containing the spread of the virus, the vulnerability that India faces is still high. As currently, nearly more than 100 cases have been reported all across India. COVID-19 is spread via airborne droplets (sneeze or cough) or contact with the surface. It is possible that a person can get COVID-19 by touching their own nose, eyes or mouth.

India is highly vulnerable due to the large population constantly travelling and working in urban agglomerations like Delhi-NCR and Mumbai. Public hygiene in India is poor despite the Swachh Bharat Abhiyan (Clean India Movements).

As we grapple with the global COVID-19 anxiety and fear, unfortunately, people tend to rely on social media platforms where rumours spread faster than the virus. The United Nations Conference on Trade and Development (UNCTAD), said the virus outbreak could cost the global economy up to $ 2 trillion this year and that the pandemic could cause a recession in some countries causing global economic growth to clock in between 2.5 % .

The Indian government is facing the twin challenge of containing the virus when the economy is already in the slowdown.

On 24 March 2020, the government of India under Prime Minister Narendra Modi ordered a nationwide lockdown for 21 days, limiting movement of the entire 1.3 billion population of India as a preventive measure towards the 2020 coronavirus pandemic in India. It was ordered after a 14 hour voluntary public curfew on 22ndMarch 2020, followed by enforcement of a series of regulations in the country's COVID-19 affected regions.

The lockdown restricts people from stepping out of their homes. All transport services – road, air and rail were suspended with exceptions for transportation of essential goods, fire, police and emergency services. Educational institutions, industrial establishments and hospitality services were also suspended. Services such as food shops, banks and ATMs, petrol pumps, other essentials and their manufacturing are exempted. The Home Ministry said that anyone who fails to follow the restrictions can face up to a year in jail.

As soon as the announcement of lockdown was made, people across the country resorted to panic buying to stock essentials despite Prime Minister's assurance of their supply. Amazon India and Flipkart temporarily suspended their services after the lockdown. Food delivery schemes were banned by several state governments despite central government's approval. Thousands of people emigrated out of major Indian cities, as they became jobless after the lockdown.

HenkBekedam, WHO representative to India praised the response describing it as "timely, comprehensive and robust." WHO executive director, Mike Ryan said that lockdowns alone will not eliminate coronavirus. He said that India must take necessary measures to prevent the second and third wave of infections.

CHAPTER VII

Conclusion and Suggestions

Research by the scientists from the United States, Europe, China, Japan and the World Health Organisation (WHO) show no certain origin of the coronavirus (COVID-19) despite Wuhan first reported the outbreak.

Although Wuhan first reported the COVID-19 outbreak, there is no evidence that China is the source of the virus. Chinese people are also victims of the virus. Because this is a new virus, there are still things that we do not know, like how severe the illness can be, how well it spreads between people and other features of the virus. There is currently no vaccine to prevent the COVID-19 infection during the initial years of the outbreak of the COVID-19 pandemic as of 2019-20.

Basic protective measures against the new coronavirus (COVID-19) are:-

- Washing hands frequently: Regularly and thoroughly cleaning our hands with an alcohol based hand rub or washing them with soap and water kills the viruses that may be in our hands.
- Maintain social distancing: Maintaining at least 1 metre or 3 feet distance between a person and another who is coughing or sneezing. When someone coughs or sneezes they spray small liquid droplets from their nose or mouth which may contain virus. If a person is too close, he can breathe in the droplets, including the COVID-19 virus if the person coughing has the disease.

- Avoid touching eyes, nose and mouth: Hands touch many surfaces and can pick up viruses. Once contaminated, hands can transfer the virus to our eyes, nose or mouth. From there, the virus can enter our body and can make us sick.
- Practice respiratory hygiene: This means covering our mouth and nose with our bent elbow or tissue when we cough or sneeze. Then dispose of the used tissue immediately. Droplets spread virus. Following good respiratory hygiene will protect the people from viruses such as cold, flu and COVID-19.
- Seek early medical care in case of fever, cough and difficulty in breathing: Calling medical care in advance will allow health care provider to quickly direct us to the right health facility. This will also protect us and help prevent spread of viruses and other infections.